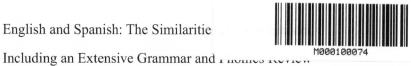

English and Spanish: The Similaritie

Including an Extensive Grammar and Phonics Review

By Scott Paulson

Copyright 2020 Scott F. Paulson

Second Edition

Dedication

To my students.

Table of Contents

Introduction

A great number of similarities and differences between the English and Spanish languages exist. Learning one of these two languages from the other one is not as difficult as a native English or Spanish speaker finds in learning many other foreign languages. Even when there are differences between English and Spanish, the differences are often slight. Concentrating on the similarities and the differences between the languages assists a language learner greatly in learning either language. This writing begins with the many similarities between English and Spanish, and then it details the differences between the two languages.

The author of this book taught English as a Second Language (ESL) students for approximately a decade at the end of a four-decade teaching career. He found that comparing the two languages was very beneficial in helping language learners learn English faster and much more effectively than they had previously been learning by only concentrating on English as a new language to them. Equally, through his personal experience, he found that Spanish is learned much easier and faster by an English speaker when making comparisons of the two languages. In other words, learning is more difficult when educators and programs insist on total immersion of a language while ignoring the incredible advantages of making comparisons. To become the best possible learned speaker, writer, and reader of either language, study beyond the philosophies of immersion is necessary. A great amount of benefit results as students concentrate on what is the same between their first language and the other language because it teaches the learner that he or she already knows much about the new language. He or she already knows the elements of the new language that are integrated with his or her own language. The language student needs to learn these integral or essential parts to learn more quickly and more efficiently. Finally, being able to speak a new language makes one's life better in many ways as it greatly increases the number of people with whom a person can communicate. Enjoy learning, as it does a person and his or her mind a great deal of good.

Scott Paulson has two other books about the English and Spanish languages, which are:

- English to Spanish Translations for Contemporary Conversation
- Christmas Words and Phrases in English and Spanish: Palabras y Frases Navideñas en Inglés y Español

About the Author

Scott Paulson is an author and English teacher who received his Bachelor of Arts degree and Illinois teaching certificate to teach secondary learners of Language Arts at North Central College in Naperville, Illinois. Of importance to this text, for more than a decade at the end of his 41-year teaching career, he taught many Spanish-speaking students who were learning English in developmental English classes as well as in English as a Second Language classes. He completed a two-year Spanish language program at the College of DuPage in Glen Ellyn, Illinois. The knowledge obtained in the classes enabled him to communicate with and relate to his students much more effectively. As he learned Spanish, he noticed the many similarities between English and Spanish and documented them in detail. He also documented the differences between Spanish and English that made learning Spanish challenging. In an effort to educate his students better, he has shared his knowledge regarding the similarities and differences with them. In this text, he shares his findings with the readers of his book. Besides writing "English and Spanish: The Similarities and Differences," he has written "70 Life's Lessons" which is an update of "65 Life's Lessons: The Most Important Lesson from Each Year of My Life," a self-explanatory book title, and "Walk – Don't Run," a young adult fiction book with historical accuracy about a young boy growing up in Joliet, Illinois, in 1960, which will entertain readers of all ages.

Since the first publication of this book in 2017, Paulson has written many other books. He has written "Instrumentals: The Number One Instrumental Recordings from 1950 - Present," which tells a great deal of information about every instrumental recording that has reached number one on Billboard's popular music charts since 1950, including informative researched facts and trivia about the songs, the recording artists, the songwriters, and much more. He wrote "My Family Won't Read My Books: About Venting Emotions," which tells the pros and cons involved in venting one's personal angers and frustrations, according to the vast research he has done on the topic. The whimsical title reveals one of his personal frustrations from the past, and in the book, he reveals how he personally has handled some of his own frustrations in life. "Restaurant Stories" is a book about some of the dining experiences he has had through the years, as he has had many. He goes into detail about his good and bad dining experiences, which entertains and informs. The text includes numbered lists of his favorite and least favorite restaurants. "My Life as a Song: The History of Recorded Music," is a historical fiction book about the life of a popular song that was fictionally born in 1892 and is still alive in the 2000s. The book takes the song, and the book's readers, through every possible form of music recordings occurring in the past century-and-a-quarter. "Food Delivery Tales: True Stories about Delivering Restaurant Food (including How to Get a Delivery Job)," is a book in which the author tells his most interesting true stories about delivered restaurant food in Chicago for several years. The book also tells perspective delivery persons what is required of obtaining such employment.

With the success of "English and Spanish: The Similarities and Differences (including an Extensive Grammar and Phonics Review)," Paulson has written a second book about the English and Spanish languages. His book, "Christmas Words and Phrases in English and Spanish: Palabras y Frases Navideñas en Inglés y Español," translates more than 400 Christmas and seasonal words and phrases, including popular song titles of the holiday season, from English to Spanish and vice versa. The first part of the book alphabetically lists the words and phrases in English and translates them to Spanish; the second part of the book alphabetically lists the words and phrases in Spanish and translates them to English.

Paulson's other English and Spanish language book is "English to Spanish Translations for Contemporary Conversation." In this book, a reader and Spanish language reader will find translations of words and phrases useful for conversing with Spanish speakers from Latin American countries, including Mexico. From basic greetings to vocabulary needed when discussing popular contemporary topics to the raw street language spoken and heard among Spanish speakers, the translations are in this book.

Chapter One: Similarities

There are major similarities between English and Spanish. Knowing everything that is identical or very similar to both languages accelerates and simplifies the learning of either language when a student's native language is Spanish or English.

For starters, both English and Spanish use the Roman alphabet, which means there are no new letters to learn. Beyond the appearance of the symbols used to spell words in both languages, the sounds are identical in most instances and very similar in others. (See Appendix 1.) Characters used to write numbers - which are 1, 2, 3, 4, 5, 6, 7, 8, 9, and 0 – are the same in both languages, as well. Up to 40 percent of the words in one language have an identical or similar word in the other language. A word that is similar or identical in both languages is called a cognate. (See Appendix 2.) The word cognate is a word that has the same linguistic derivation as another word because it is from the same original word or root. Therefore, by knowing either language, a language learner only has approximately 60 percent of the words that still need to be learned. Therefore, the more-than-a-thousand words that are cognates in English and Spanish are obviously easy to learn. Students only need to know which words they already know in their native language are cognates. However, there are false cognates, also called false friends, which can confuse learners. (Appendix 3.) The false cognates need to be learned, too. An example of a false cognate is the word 'actual' which means 'existing in fact' in English but means 'currently' in Spanish. Another false cognate is the English word 'embarrassed' which looks much like the Spanish word 'embarazada.' In English, 'embarrassed' means 'to make uncomfortably self-conscious' while 'embarazada' means 'pregnant' in Spanish.

***

Though all 26 letters in the English alphabet also exist in the Spanish alphabet, a-b-c-d-e-f-g-h-i-j-k-l-m-n-o-p-q-r-s-t-u-v-w-x-y-z, there is a difference in Spanish. The difference is that the Spanish letters sometimes include a different marking besides the letter that stands alone. For example, in addition to the letter n, there is an ñ in Spanish; the two have different sounds. Additionally, vowels sometimes have a marking above them. The accent marks on vowels either indicate where an emphasis or stress should be sounded within a word, or the accent mark can distinguish two different words that are spelled with the same letters. For example, 'si' without the accent above the i means 'if' and 'sí' with the accent above the i means 'yes.'

***

As far as the sounds of the letters, the biggest difference is that the five vowels - a, e, i, o, u – basically have five distinctive sounds in Spanish. (See Appendix 4.) The same five vowels in English have 12 sounds. Vowels, of course, are extremely important in English and Spanish because almost every word has a vowel when the letter y is also considered a vowel. Beyond every word having a vowel, every syllable in every word has a vowel.

***

Another difference is that English has eight to ten diphthongs. Specifically, there are eight according to A.C. Gimson, nine according to J.D. O'Connor, and 10 according to Daniel Jones. In contrast, Spanish has five diphthongs. The word diphthong means double sound or double tone. Therefore, diphthongs are usually two vowels placed next to each other in a word that make two distinctive sounds. An example of a diphthong in English is the word 'actual' as one pronounces both the u and the second a, which are side-by-side in the written word. An example of a diphthong in Spanish is the name 'Juan' as one pronounces both the 'u' and the 'a' which are side-by-side in the written word. There are diphthongs, or two vowel sounds heard simultaneously in words that do not have two vowels written side by side, such as the English word 'ride.' To explain, even though there is only one vowel written between the 'r' and the 'd' in the word 'ride,' two vowel sounds are pronounced between the 'r' and the 'd,' which gives the word a diphthong.

There are three major diphthongs in English, as they involve large movements of the tongue and are common in words consisting of diphthongs. The three are the 'ai' sound as heard in the English word 'ride,' the 'ow' sound as heard in the word 'loud,' and the 'oi' sound as heard in 'noise.'

The opposite of a diphthong is a monophthong, which is a single vowel sound. A monophthong is more common in speaking either English or Spanish.

***

Additionally, in English, letters are sometimes silent in words while the letter h is the only silent letter in Spanish. Consider the English word 'though' in which the last three letters are not pronounced. In Spanish, consider the word 'hola', which means 'hello' in English; the first letter is silent. English is considered difficult to spell with its many rules as compared to Spanish, which, for the most part, has one letter for each sound in a word. Exceptions are when two letters make one sound, such as sh-, th-, and ch-, which are found in both languages. The letter combinations of sh. th, and ch, are much more common in English words than in Spanish.

***

If you are knowledgeable of grammar in either language, you know the grammar of both languages because they are similar. Grammar has eight parts of speech, which are noun, pronoun, verb, adjective, adverb, conjunction, preposition, and interjection. Some break tradition and refer to articles and determiners as two more parts of speech. Traditionalist, however, insist there are eight parts of speech, and refer to articles and determiners as adjectives or modifiers. In English and Spanish, every word falls into one of the eight parts of speech. (Appendix 5.)

***

Learners will find that sentence structure is similar in English and Spanish, as the subject most commonly precedes the predicate. At times, however, Spanish sentences omit the pronoun as the subject of the sentence because it is not needed to distinguish the pronoun. The pronoun at the beginning of the sentence is unnecessary because the form of the verb in the sentence indicates the pronoun. Incidentally, the subject of a sentence is who or what the sentence is about, and its counterpart, the predicate, either tells what happens to the subject of the sentence or tells something else about the subject of the sentence. Additionally, in most instances, the word order in sentences is similar or the same in both languages. However, this is an aspect of writing and speaking that is also covered in this book's section about the languages' differences, as there is usually a major difference in word order in relation to the nouns and their adjectives. In English, the adjective precedes the noun; in Spanish, the noun almost always precedes the adjective.

***

Capitalization and punctuation in the written forms of the two languages are usually the same, but there are some differences discussed in Chapter Two. Primarily, the differences in punctuation involve numbers (the use of commas versus periods in writing numbers), while the capitalization differences need to be studied for one to write correctly. For example, the names of months and days are capitalized in English but not capitalized in Spanish.

***

One other similarity of the two languages is actually a difference within each language. Each language has different types within itself. In other words, depending where a person is from in an English-speaking or Spanish-speaking country, some word usages and sounds – or accents – often differ. For example, some of the words and sounds spoken in Spanish as it is spoken in Spain are sometimes different that the Spanish spoken is Mexico and other Latin American countries. In fact, there are such specific differences that people from different parts of the Spanish-speaking world can decipher which area of a country a person comes from. This is because some of the words a person uses, as well as the sounds or accents a person produces, are locally distinct. Equally, some of the words and sounds an English speaker produces may differ from what is spoken by an English-speaker in a different part of the world. For example, there is a noticeable difference in some of the words used and the sounds produced when comparing an English speaker from the United States to an English speaker from England. Even more specifically, people from a particular country can sometimes tell which part of the country another native speaker comes from due to the words the person uses and the accent in which he or she speaks.

Just as the colloquialisms a person uses may decipher where he or she may come from within the United States, the way a person speaks Spanish can suggest the part of Mexico or Latin America he or she comes from, as well. In this book, the English language references are the English commonly spoken and understood throughout the United States. The Spanish language references in this book are based on the Spanish commonly spoken by persons who live in, or have come to the United States from, Mexico or one of Mexico's nearby Latin American countries.

***

A final comment on the benefits of learning English from Spanish or Spanish from English by noting the similarities as well as the differences between the languages:

While there are programs and schools that insist in total immersion of a language being taught, there are educators and others who strongly believe it is a disservice to language learners when the comparisons of the two languages are disallowed. Denying the teaching of similarities and differences between English and Spanish is very possibly a defensive move on the part of an educator who does not know the native language of the students he or she is teaching. That deficiency on the part of some educators should not be a reason to stop teachers, who know both languages, from teaching the similarities as well as noting the confusing differences between the two languages. Again, I have seen the teaching of the similarities and differences among English and Spanish to be a great asset to the students who will ultimately know both languages. In particular, I repeat, teaching the commonalities between the two languages is extremely assistive in the language learning process. Explaining a similarity often clarifies something within a language lesson to a student. Being aware of the similarities saves a student a great deal of time and frustration in learning. It also saves a teacher time and frustration from needlessly explaining a language concept from scratch when it can easily be exemplified for students by making a comparative reference to the students' already-learned native language. Moreover, when a teacher isn't forced to immerse a student into a new language and is allowed to reference a student's native language academically, a student can be delightfully enlightened and less intimidated by the new language. As the student realizes how much he or she already knows about the new language being taught to him or her, it simplifies learning. It also simplifies teaching. These assertions can't be denied.

***

To summarize Chapter One, the similarities between English and Spanish primarily include the symbols and characters used to write letters and numbers, the phonetic sounds often made when pronouncing words, the word cognates, the grammar including the parts of speech, the sentence structure, the word order in most instances, and a similar characteristic of having many variations of the two languages throughout the globe.

There are some differences between the English and Spanish languages that make learning either language more difficult. Knowing these differences in the beginning stages of the language learning process is extremely beneficial. Just as knowing everything that is identical or very similar to both languages accelerates and simplifies the learning of either language, knowing the difficult, troublesome, or tricky differences between the two languages accelerates and simplifies language learning as well.

***

Word order in spoken and written English and Spanish is occasionally different, as mentioned previously in Chapter One. The big difference is the placement of adjectives (the words that describe nouns) in relation to the nouns (which are the names of a person, place, thing, or idea). In English, adjectives are most often put before the nouns they modify while adjectives in Spanish are most often put after nouns. For example, one says 'the big boy' in English while, in Spanish, one says 'el chico grande,' which is literally 'the boy big' because 'chico' is the word for 'boy in Spanish and 'grande' is the word for 'big' in Spanish.

***

Grammatical differences involve the use of auxiliary verbs in English, which are sometimes absent in spoken and written Spanish. Auxiliary verbs are used with action verbs to form the tenses of the action verbs (present, past, future) as well as the moods and voices of other verbs. The basic auxiliary verbs are the verb forms of 'be' (am, is, are, was, were, being, been), 'do' (does, do, did), and 'have' (has, have, had, having). Some auxiliary verbs are modal and never change their form (can, could, may, might, must, ought, shall, should, will, would). The English verbs 'be,' 'do,' and 'have' may be used alone as well as an auxiliary, which means it can accompany an action word to comprise a verb phrase. Incidentally, a phrase contains more than one word as opposed to a single word. For example, in the sentence 'I am tall,' the verb 'am' is alone because there is no action verb following it. The word 'tall' after the verb 'am' describes the subject, which is "I." Therefore, 'tall' is an adjective and not a verb. In the sentence 'I am walking,' the verb is the verb phrase 'am walking,' because 'am' is an auxiliary verb preceding 'walking,' which is an action verb.

For our purposes, we can compare the question 'do you eat at home?' in both languages. In English the auxiliary verb 'do' must be used. Contrarily, 'do' is not present in Spanish, 'comes en casa?' which is literally 'you eat at home?' The Spanish word 'comes' means 'you eat.' In English, the form of a verb does not necessarily distinguish what the subject of a sentence. Contrarily, the form of a verb does distinguish the subject of a sentence in Spanish. Therefore, the auxiliary verb is most often dropped when speaking or writing questions in Spanish. The English verb 'do' in such questions as 'do you eat at home?' is always dropped in Spanish. In fact, the English word 'do' as an auxiliary verb doesn't even exist in Spanish.

***

Another huge difference is Spanish and English grammar is the huge amount of prepositions that are used in English that are not found in Spanish. In Spanish, one preposition such as 'en' can mean 'in,' 'on,' or 'at' in English. The very common Spanish preposition 'a' can mean 'at,' 'by,' 'for,' or 'by' in English. The Spanish preposition 'sobre' means 'about,' 'above,' 'around,' 'on,' 'over,' or 'upon' in English. Another very common Spanish preposition, 'de,' can mean 'from,' 'of,' or 'with' in English. Therefore, Spanish speakers who are learning English have to learn many more prepositions than they use in Spanish to communicate correctly and understandably in English.

***

Another difference between Spanish and English is that Spanish nouns have gender and English nouns do not. This means that the article preceding a noun alternates in Spanish. An article is a word that modifies a noun, which is a person, place, thing, or idea. The articles 'a,' 'an,' and 'the' are basic in English as they are placed before nouns. The article 'a' and 'an' are for non-specific nouns and the article 'the' is for specific nouns. For example, if one asks for a pencil, the person wants any pencil; if one asks for the pencil, the person is asking for a specific pencil. The difference between 'a' and 'an' is that 'a' precedes a word that begins with a consonant sound and 'an' precedes a noun that begins with a vowel sound. For example, it is correct to say 'a pencil' and to say 'an ink pen.'

In Spanish, more articles are needed to satisfy the gender attached to the nouns. The articles are assigned by a noun's gender rather than whether it is a specific or non-specific noun. The Spanish articles are 'el,' 'la,' 'los,' and 'las.' 'El' accompanies the masculine nouns and 'la' accompanies the female nouns. For the most part, masculine nouns end in the letter o and feminine nouns end in the letter a. For example, 'the boy' is 'el chico' in Spanish as it is masculine; 'the girl' is 'la chica' in Spanish as it is feminine. As in English, the letter 's' is usually placed at the end of the plural forms of nouns in Spanish. In Spanish, plurals are also indicated in the articles as 'el' becomes 'los' for plural nouns that are masculine and 'la' becomes 'las' for plural nouns that are feminine. Therefore, 'the boys' becomes 'los chicos' in Spanish and 'the girls' becomes 'las chicas' in Spanish. Notice that an 's' is added to 'chico' and 'chica' to make the words plural just as an 's' is added to 'boy' and 'girl' to make the words plural in English. Besides an article before a noun, any modifiers associated with a noun reflect the masculine or feminine gender as well as its plurality. For example, 'the tall boy' is 'el chico alto' in Spanish and 'the tall boys' is 'los chicos altos.' Notice how, in Spanish, the adjectives 'alto' and 'altos' are placed after the nouns it describes rather than before the nouns, as in done in English. 'The tall girl' is 'la chica alta' in Spanish and 'the tall girls' is 'las chicas altas.' Again, when the nouns become a different gender and change from singular to plural, the adjectives change, too.

This is one aspect of Spanish that makes Spanish more difficult than English because, again, English does not have genders for words. Incidentally, a few Spanish words have unexpected genders as they do not always follow the rules regarding the noun's last letter. Examples of such gender-assigned nouns in Spanish are 'el dia' and 'la foto.' 'Dia,' the Spanish word for 'day,' appears to be feminine because it ends in the letter 'a' but is masculine. 'Foto,' the Spanish word for 'photo,' appears to be masculine because it ends in the letter 'o' but is feminine. The reason for 'foto' being feminine is that it is a short form of the feminine word 'fotografía,' which translates to photograph in English. Again, the last letter of the Spanish noun does not always accurately suggest whether the word is masculine or feminine. The challenging articles followed by a gender-specific noun have to be memorized for writing and speaking Spanish correctly.

***

Though there are many similarities between English and Spanish regarding the capitalization of words - such as capitalizing the first word in a sentence, proper names of people and pets, and the proper names of places like countries and cities - there are some differences when Spanish does not capitalize a word as it is properly capitalized in English. Some of the instances when a word is capitalized in English but not Spanish include the names of the days of the week, the names of the months of the year, the names of religions, and the names of nationalities. Additionally, while the first person singular pronoun 'I' is always capitalized in English, its Spanish equivalent, which is 'yo,' is not capitalized unless it is capitalized for another reason such as being the first word in a sentence.

***

Similarly, though punctuation (the period, comma, question mark, quotation marks, and exclamation point) is similar in both English and Spanish, there are a couple of important differences as to when they are used. Most prominent is the changing of the period for the comma when writing numbers. In English one-thousand is written with a comma (1,000) while in Spanish it is written with a period (1.000). When writing one-and-a-half numerically in English, one uses the period between the 1 and the 5 (1.5) and in most Spanish-speaking countries a comma is used to numerically write one-and-a-half (1,5).

In Spanish, an inverted question mark (¿) is placed before an interrogative sentence – a sentence that asks a question - and the right-side up question mark (?) is placed at the end of it. In English, there is no punctuation mark before an interrogative sentence; there is only a right-side up question mark at the end of the question. Likewise, in Spanish, an exclamatory sentence has punctuation at the beginning and the end of the sentence. An inverted exclamation point (¡) precedes an exclamatory sentence and a right-side up exclamation point (!) is placed at the end of the sentence. In English, no exclamation point precedes exclamatory sentences; there is only a right-side up exclamation point at the end. Also, the inverted punctuation in Spanish may come somewhere in the middle of a sentence if the first word or first words of the sentence are not part of the question or exclamation. In some instances in Spanish, one may see a form of an exclamation point and a question mark in the same sentence. In written Spanish, an inverted question mark or an inverted exclamation point within a sentence as opposed to being at either end of a sentence does not need a capital letter following the punctuation mark.

Chapter Three: Spanish Speakers' Common Mistakes

Beware of common mistakes made by Spanish speakers learning English. These errors include pronunciation errors. At times, Spanish speakers do not pronounce the end consonant of English words (such as saying 'car' instead of 'card') or do not pronounce those sounds correctly (such as saying 'think' instead of 'thing'). These errors can cause confusion for people who are trying to understand the spoken English words. Beyond confusing, it can cause miscommunication among people.

***

The 'v' sound is foreign to Spanish speakers. Regarding the 'v' sound, a person forms his or her mouth like the Disney character Bugs Bunny by putting the front upper teeth over the lower lip and then says v-v-valentines as most of people have heard of Valentine's Day. The 'v' sound is actually the voiced 'f' sound, which means a person can think of pronouncing a 'v' like pronouncing an 'f' but adding more vocal sound to it.

***

There is a great tendency for Spanish speakers to mispronounce words that begin with the letter as well as the sound 's.' Native Spanish speakers sometimes say 'es' – adding a short 'e' sound before the 's' sound. Most of the time, this error occurs when there is a consonant after an s at the beginning of the word. For example, they sometimes say the non-existent word 'eschool' instead of the word 'school.' Sometimes they see a name like 'Scott' and pronounce it 'escott' or 'escot' with a 'long o' vowel sound instead of a 'soft o.' This confusion is most likely caused because the Spanish equivalent of these English words starting with the letter 's' often begin with the letters 'es' in Spanish. For example, the English word 'school' is 'escuela' in Spanish, the English word 'stupid' is 'estúpido' in Spanish, and the English word 'studying' is 'estudiando' in Spanish, and the English word 'student' is 'estudiante' in Spanish. Consider English words starting with the letter s to be the initial sound in some common Spanish words such as 'sábado' which is Spanish for the English word 'Saturday' or 'salsa' which is Spanish for the English word 'sauce,' while also being a common English word.

***

Finally, deleting consonant sounds in consonant clusters is sometimes problematic for new English speakers who come from a Spanish-speaking background. For example, instead of saying the English word 'cluster,' a person may say 'clusser.' Such errors make a listener's ability to comprehend a speaker challenging.

***

Finally, the 'th' sound in English is extremely difficult for some Spanish speakers to pronounce, even though the sound that is usually made in Spanish when the letter d is between two vowel sounds in Spanish is the same. In English, there are two 'th' sounds: the unvoiced, voiceless, or 'soft th' as in the word 'thin' and the 'voiced or hard th' as in the word 'that.' Spanish speakers tend to pronounce the unvoiced 'th' incorrectly as the letter 't.' For example, when meaning to say 'thin,' a person may say 'tin' or meaning to say 'teeth' and saying 'teet' instead. 'Teet,' incidentally, is not an English word.

***

The 'z' sound as it is pronounced in English does not exist in Spanish. In Latin American Spanish, the letter z is pronounced with the 's' sound. Elsewhere, such as in Spain, the 'z' sound is pronounced with the 'unvoiced or soft th' sound.

The 'z' sound is basically a voiced 's' sound because the mouth forms the same way to make an 's' sound as it does to form a 'z' sound. Specifically, the 'z' sound is made by creating friction through one's clenched teeth and directing air beyond the tip of one's tongue. Again, it is the same as making the 's' sound but without the friction.

***

Remember that Spanish most often has a sound for every letter in a word and English often has letters that are silent. The letter h in a Spanish word is an exception as the letter h is silent in Spanish. One of the most common pronunciation errors Spanish speakers make is pronouncing the silent e at the end of English words. An example of this error occurred when I was speaking to a man who recently arrived from Mexico and told me that he was lost and needed to find Kedvale Avenue. Though I understood his Spanish, I did not initially understand the name of the street he wanted to find. He repeatedly said that he was looking for 'Kedbalay.' Beyond incorrectly pronouncing the English letter v as the 'b' sound, he also pronounced the silent e at the end of the word as a Spanish speaker pronounces the letter e at the end of a Spanish word. Again, English has many words with silent letters, and the silent letters often give direction as to how other letters are pronounced in the word. In the street name Kedvale, the silent e at the end of the word tells the speaker of the word that the letter a is pronounced as a long 'a' sound as opposed to one of the other sounds that the letter 'a' makes in English.

***

Finally, as suggested above, one needs to study the many vowel sounds that exist in English. Not only are some vowels pronounced differently in English than they are pronounced in Spanish, but vowels have many more pronunciation possibilities in English than they have in Spanish. One of the most often-heard errors in pronunciation from Spanish speakers is when the letter i appears in the middle of a word. Because the letter i in Spanish is pronounced like the long 'e' sound in English, a word like 'ship' is mispronounced as sheep. Such errors in pronunciation cause difficulty in being understood by a listener. Such errors can also cause people to miscommunicate.

***

While Spanish commonly uses double negatives in their speaking and writing, using double negatives English is bad grammar. In Spanish, making something negative is easy by usually just putting the word 'no' before the word being made negative; but in English, words often become negative by forming a new word by putting one of several prefixes before the base of the word being made negative. For example, instead of saying or writing 'not like, one often uses the word 'dislike' by attaching 'dis' to the front of the word 'like.' Other examples are to say 'inability' to indicate that someone or something does not have 'ability,' to indicate that something is 'not essential' by using the word 'nonessential,' and to indicate that someone or something is not satisfactory by using the word 'unsatisfactory.' However, words that have prefixes in both languages often have similar prefixes, such as the English and Spanish word equivalents of 'prefix' in English and 'prefijo' in Spanish, and 'supermarket' in English and 'supermercado' in Spanish.

***

Finally, false cognates, or false friends, which are Spanish words that look like English words but mean something different, also cause confusion and errors by Spanish speakers who are learning English. (Appendix 3.)

Chapter Four: English Speakers' Common Mistakes

Beware of common mistakes made by English speakers learning Spanish. These errors include pronunciation errors in that Spanish has some consonants that have different sounds than the English letter equivalent. Also, Spanish basically has one sound per letter, including the vowels. In English, of course, all five vowels have numerous sounds in English. A common mistake among English speakers speaking Spanish is to give the vowels in Spanish the incorrect sound. When unsure of which sound a vowel should have in Spanish, it is best to use the vowel sound most often, if not always, associated with the vowel in Spanish. Naturally, to be understood by Spanish speakers, time spent studying and practicing the sounds associated with every letter in the Spanish alphabet is beneficial. (Appendix 1 in this book has all of the Spanish letters' sounds detailed.)

***

Errors made by persons speaking Spanish while have English as their first language include the grammatical use of correct gender forms of nouns and adjectives. This needs to be learned since there are no gender forms of nouns and adjectives in English. It is one of the few elements of the Spanish language that can make learning Spanish more difficult than learning English.

***

Grammatically, the common word order of an adjective and the noun it modifies can confuse a native English speaker when learning Spanish. While the noun almost always follows its adjectives in English, the nouns most always precede the adjectives in Spanish. For example, in English, 'cold day' places the adjective 'cold' before the noun 'day.' The Spanish translation of 'cold day' is 'día frío.' The Spanish word 'día' translates to 'day' in English, and the Spanish word 'frío' translates to 'cold' in Spanish. Therefore, a literal translation of 'cold day' in English becomes 'day cold' in Spanish.

***

The subject of sentences, which is always used in English, is often dropped in Spanish. The reason for dropping the pronoun in Spanish is because it becomes redundant. The verb form in Spanish reveals the subject pronoun of a sentence. Examples of pronoun subjects being dropped are seen in the statements 'I eat' and 'you eat.' The infinitive of 'eat' in English is 'to eat.' The infinitive of 'eat' in Spanish is 'comer.' (Incidentally, an infinitive in English is the word 'to' followed by the verb.) As is obvious in this example, the verb doesn't change in English when one says or writes 'I eat' and 'you eat.' The verb 'eat' doesn't change whether the subject is 'I' or 'you.' Therefore, the pronouns 'I' and 'you' are necessary to distinguish the subject. However, in Spanish, the verb 'comer' becomes 'yo como' for 'I eat' and 'tú comes' for 'you eat.' Since the verb form changes, depending on what the subject is, one deciphers the subject of the sentence by the verb form. 'Como' means exactly the same as 'yo como,' and 'comes' means exactly the same as 'tú comes.' Therefore, in such examples, 'yo' and 'tú' are not needed. Furthermore, they are most often dropped by Spanish speakers.

***

In Spanish, there are two singular forms of the pronoun 'you.' Using the wrong form can be considered impolite or awkward. The two forms are 'tú' and 'usted.' 'Tú' is informal and should be used when addressing people who are friends or who are younger. 'Usted' is formal and should be used when speaking to an older person or when speaking to an authoritative person. When uncertain as to which 'you' form to use, it is best to address the person with 'usted.' Another difference with the second person pronoun 'you' is that English uses the same word, 'you,' for singular and plural. Whether speaking directly to one person or more than one person, 'you' is the correct pronoun. In Spanish, however, there is a separate word for the plural 'you,' which is 'ustedes.' Again, while there is only one word for 'you' in English, there are three in Spanish, which are 'tú,' 'usted,' and 'ustedes.'

***

While there is one 'to be' verb in English, there are two forms of the 'to be' verb in Spanish. This can cause great confusion to learners of the Spanish language. The two forms of 'to be' in Spanish are 'ser' and 'estar.' 'Ser' is used for a permanent state of being such as one's appearance, one's employment, and permanent characteristics of something. Contrarily, 'estar' is used for more flexible states of being such as one's current location or how a person currently is or feels.

A conjugation of the verb 'ser' is: 'yo soy' meaning 'I am,' 'tú eres' (informal singular) and 'usted es' (formal singular) meaning 'you are,' 'él/ella/ello/uno es' meaning 'he/she/it/one is,' 'nosotros somos' meaning 'we are,' 'ustedes son' (plural) meaning 'you are,' 'ellos/ellas son' meaning 'they (masculine)/they (feminine) are.'

Regarding the 'ellos' and 'ellas' as the Spanish pronouns used for the English pronoun 'they,' 'ellos' is the masculine form and should be used whether one or all persons being addressed are male. 'Ellas' is only used when all persons in a group are female.

A conjugation of the verb 'estar' is: 'yo estoy' meaning 'I am,' 'tú estás' (informal singular) and 'usted estás' (formal singular) meaning 'you are,' 'él/ella/ello/uno está' meaning 'he/she/it/one is,' 'nosotros estamos' meaning 'we are,' 'ustedes están' (plural) meaning 'you are,' 'ellos/ellas están' meaning 'they (masculine)/they (feminine) are.'

Again, the 'ellos' and 'ellas' Spanish pronouns used for the English pronoun 'they' differentiates by gender with 'ellos' being the masculine form and 'ellas' being the feminine form.

It takes study and practice to use the correct 'to be' verbs in Spanish. Though using 'ser' when 'estar' is correct, or vice versa, Spanish speakers will likely understand a non-native speaker who may use the incorrect form.

***

Unlike English words, many Spanish words have accent marks on vowels, which either indicate where an emphasis should be placed on a sound within a word or distinguish two different words that are spelled with the same letters. For example, the Spanish word 'si,' without the accent above the letter i, means 'if' in English, and the Spanish word 'sí,' with an accent above the letter i means 'yes' in English.

***

Finally, false cognates, or false friends, which are English words that look like Spanish words but mean something different, cause confusion and errors by English speakers who are learning Spanish. (Appendix 3.)

Appendix 1

The Spanish Letters' Sounds (as pronounced in Spanish in most locations, particularly in Mexico and Latin American countries)

A is pronounced 'ah,' as the letter 'a' is pronounced in the English word 'mama'

B is pronounced as a 'soft b' in pronounced in the English word 'bit'

C has two Spanish pronunciations as it does in English; it is pronounced as the letter 'k' is pronounced in the English word 'car,' but is pronounced as the letter 's' in the English word 'center' when the letter c is before the letter e or i

D has two Spanish pronunciations; besides being pronounced the same as the letter 'd' is pronounced in English, as in the English word 'dog;' in Spanish, it is also pronounced as a 'soft th' as in the English word 'thing' when the d is between two vowels in a Spanish word

E is most often pronounced as a 'long a' is pronounced in the English word 'bake,' but is sometimes pronounced as the English exclamation 'eh'

F is pronounced the same as the letter 'f' is pronounced in English, as in the English word 'find'

G has two Spanish pronunciations as it does in English; besides being pronounced the same with a 'hard g' as in the English word 'gift,' it is also pronounced as it is in English with an 'h' sound when it is before an e or i, as in the English word 'heavy'

H is 'silent' unless the word is adopted from another language, such as the word 'Hawaii'

I is pronounced as a 'long e' as in the English word 'sleep'

J is pronounced as an 'h' in the English word 'hello'

K, a letter rarely used in Spanish, is pronounced as a 'k' in the English word 'cake'

L is pronounced the same as the letter 'l' is pronounced in English, as in the English word 'like'

M is pronounced the same as the letter 'm' is pronounced in English, as in the English word 'milk'

N is pronounced the same as the letter 'n' is pronounced in English, as in the English word 'nice'

O is pronounced as a 'long o' is pronounced in English, as in the English word 'only'

P is pronounced the same as the letter 'p' is pronounced in English, as in the English word 'people'

Q is pronounced as the letter 'k' is pronounced in the English word 'king;' in Spanish, the letter 'q' is always followed by the letter 'u' as in the English word 'quick'

R has various Spanish pronunciations; besides the 'r' sound, it is often perceived as a 'soft d,' as in the English word 'dig;' at the beginning of a Spanish word, the r is trilled to sound like a repetitive t sound, of which there is no equivalent English sound

S is pronounced the same as the letter 's' is pronounced in English, as in the English word 'sand'

T is pronounced as a 'soft t' as in the English word 'tin'

U is pronounced 'oo' as in the English word 'moon'

V is pronounced as a 'soft b' as in the English word 'bit'

W, a letter rarely used in Spanish, is pronounced the same as the letter 'w' is pronounced in English, as in the English word 'Wi-Fi'

X is pronounced like the 'ks' as in the English word 'extra,' additionally, it sounds like an s, h or sh when it is in names

Y is pronounced the same as the letter 'y' is pronounced in English, as in the English word 'year'

Z is pronounced as an 's' in the English word 'sand'

ll (two of the letter l, side by side) is pronounced as the letter 'y' in the English word 'year '

ñ is pronounced as the combined letters 'ny' sound in English, as in the n-i portion of the English word 'onion'

rr (two of the letter r, side by side) is a 't trilled;' in English, there is no equivalent sound to the rr which is the same sound of one r that is at the beginning of a Spanish word

ch and sh letter combinations are commonly pronounced as they are in English; ch is pronounced in as in the English word 'church,' and sh is pronounced as it is in the English word 'shadow'

Appendix 2

Cognates

Cognates are words in two languages that look similar or are spelled the same and have the same definition.

***

Cognates often follow patterns in their spelling changes from English to Spanish. The following list summarizes the patterns:

English words ending in –ance change to ancia in Spanish

English words ending in –ant change to –ante in Spanish

English words ending in –ary change to –ario in Spanish

English words ending in –ct change to –cto in Spanish

English words ending in –ence change to –encia in Spanish

English words ending in –ic change to –ico in Spanish

English words ending in –id change to –ido in Spanish

English words ending in –ism change to –ismo in Spanish

English words ending in –ist change to –ista in Spanish

English words ending in –ment change to –mento in Spanish

English words ending in –ly change to –mente in Spanish

English words ending in –ous change to –ioso in Spanish

English words ending in –ology change to –ología in Spanish

English words ending in –tion change to –ción in Spanish

English words ending in –ty change to –idad or –itad in Spanish

English words that have a 'ph' in it often have an 'f' in place of the 'ph'

English words that have a 'th' in it often have a 't' without the 'h'

English words that have a double consonant within the word often only have one of the consonants in the Spanish equivalent, though the double r (rr) is common in Spanish and has a trilled-t sound of its own

English words ending in –al, -ar, and –ble are usually the same word in Spanish

There are exceptions to these spelling patterns; therefore, check a Spanish-English dictionary when uncertain.

***

Cognates (English word followed by the Spanish word equivalent): a partial list, listed alphabetically

abundant/abundante, accident/accidente, accidental/accidental, accompany/acomplañar, acid/ácido, act/acto, active/activo, activities/actividades, actor/actor, admirable/admirable, admire/admirar, admit/admitir, adopt/adoptar, adult/adulto, adventure/adventura, agenda/agenda, agent/agente, air/aire, alarm/alarma, alcohol/alcohol, alcoholic/alcohólico, altar/altar, ambulance/ambulancia, animal/animal, announce/anunciar, appear/aparecer, appetite/apetito, archaeology/arqueología, area/area, argument/argumento, artificial/artificial, artist/artista, audible/audible, authority/authoridad, auto/auto, autograph/autógrafo, automobile/automóvil,

balance/balance, banana/banana, banjo/banjo, bar/bar, base/base, basic/básico, bicycle/bicicleta, blouse/blusa, bridge/bridge, brilliant/brillante, brutal/brutal,

cabin/cabina, cable/cable, cafe/café, canal/canal, canary/canario, cancer/cancer, canon/canon, capital/capital, capitalism/capitalismo, capture/capturar, carbon/carbon, casual/casual, cause/causa, celebrate/celebrar, cement/cemento, center/centro, central/central, cereal/cereal, cerebral/cerebral, ceremony/ceremonia, chimney/chimenea, chocolate/chocolate, circular/circular, class/clase, coast/costa, coincidence/coincidencia, collaborate/colaborar, colony/colonia, color/color, combustion/combustión, common/común, communism/comunismo, competence/competencia, complete/completo, concert/concierto, conclusion/conclusión, conductor/conductor, confusing/confuso, confusion/confusión, considerable/considerable, contend/contender, continent/continente, continue/continuar, contract/contrato, considerable/considerable, control/control, cordial/cordial, correct/correcto, counterattack/contraataque, coyote/coyote, crocodile/cocodrilo, criminal/criminal, crisis/crisis, cultural/cultural, curious/curioso,

debate/debate, decide/decidir, decoration/decoración, delicate/delicado, delicious/delicioso, dentist/dentista, department/departmento, depend/depender, deport/deportar, describe/describer, desert/desierto, destroy/destruir, destructible/destructible, detain/detener, determine/determinar, dialect/dialecto, diamond/diamante, diary/diario, dictator/dictador, difference/diferencia, different/diferente, difficulty/dificultad, digital/digital, dinosaur/dinosaurio, direction/dirección, directly/directamente, disappear/desaparecer, disaster/desastre, discuss/discutir, disgrace/disgracia, disobedience/disobediencía, distance/distancia, distant/distante, distribute/distribuir, division/división, doctor/doctor, document/documento, double/doble, dollar/dólar, drama/drama, dynamite/dinamita,

ecology/ecología, editorial/editorial, elegant/elegante, element/elemento, elemental/elemental, elephant/elefante, empathy/empatía, enigma/enigma, enormous/enorme, enter/entrar, error/error, escape/escapar, specially/especialmente, essence/esencia, exact/exacto, examine/examinar, excellence/excelencia, exclaim/exclamar, exclusive/exclusivo, excursion/excursión, experimental/experimental, explosion/explosión, extra/extra, expulsion/expulsión, extension/extensión, exterior/exterior, extraordinary/extraordinario,

factor/factor, faculty/facultad, familiar/familiar, family/familia, famous/famoso, fantastic/fantástico, fascinate/fascinar, fatal/fatal, favorite/favorito, federal/federal, fidelity/fidelidad, ferocious/feroz, festival/festival, final/final, finally/finalmente, firm/firme, flexible/flexible, flower/flor, fluid/fluido, formal/formal, formula/formula, fortunately/afortunademente, fraction/fracción, frontal/frontal, fruit/fruta, fundamental/fundamental, funeral/funeral, furious/furioso,

gala/gala, galaxy/galaxia, gas/gas, gene/gene, general/general, generic/genérico, geology/geología, giraffe/jirafa, global/global, glossary/glosario, golf/golf, glorious/glorioso, gorilla/gorila, graph/gráfica, group/grupo, habitual/habitual, history/historia, hobby/hobby, honor/honor, horizontal/horizontal, horror/horror, hospital/hospital, hotel/hotel, hour/hora, horrible/horrible, human/humano,

idea/idea, ideal/ideal, imagine/imaginar, immediately/inmediamente, immigrants/inmigrantes, importance/importancia, imperial/imperial, implacable/implacable, important/importante, impressed/impresionando, incurable/incurable, incursion/incursión, independence/independencia, individual/individual, industrial/industrial, inevitable/inevitable, inferior/inferior, informal/informal, insect/insecto, inseparable/inseparable, insist/insister, inspector/inspector, intelligence/inteligencia, interesting/interesante, interminable/interminable, interrupt/interrumpir, introduce/introducir, invasion/invasión, invent/inventar, investigate/investigar, invisible/invisible, invite/invitar, irregular/irregular, island/isla,

judicial/judicial,

kilo/kilo,

lateral/lateral, legal/legal, lens/lente, leopard/leopardo, liberty/libertad, list/lista, literal/literal, local/local, locate/localizar, lunar/lunar,

macho/macho, maestro/maestro, magic/magia, magician/mago, manner/manera, mango/mango, mania/manía, manual/manual, map/mapa, march/marchar, marginal/marginal, material/material, matrimonial/matrimonial, medal/medulla, medic/medico, medical/medical, medieval/medieval, mediocre/mediocre, melon/melón, memory/memoria, mental/mental, menu/menú, metal/metal, microscope/microscopio, miniature/miniatura, minute/minute, moment/momento, monument/monumento, mortal/mortal, motel/motel, motor/motor, much/mucho, multiple/múltiple, municipal/municipal, muscular/muscular, musical/musical, mysterious/misterioso,

nation/nación, natural/natural, necessity/necesidad, nervous/nervioso, noble/noble, normal/normal, nostalgia/nostalgia, note/nota, notice/noticia, numerous/numeroso,

obedience/obediencia, object/objecto, observatory/observatorio, office/oficina, opera/opera, operation/operación, oral/oral, ordinary/ordinario, oriental/oriental, original/original, palace/palacio, panorama/panorama, paper/papel, park/parque, part/parte, pasta/pasta, pastor/pastora, patience/paciencia, patio/patio, peculiar/peculiar, perfect/perfecto, permanent/permanente, personal/personal, photo/foto, piano/piano, pioneer/pionero, pirate/pirata, planet/planeta, planetarium/planetario, plans/planes, plants/plantas, plates/platos, plural/plural, popular/popular, practice/practicar, precious/precioso, prefix/prefijo, prepare/preparar, present/presentar, primary/primario, principal/principal, probable/probable, problem/problema, professional/profesional, propaganda/propaganda, protector/protector, provincial/provincial, publication/publicación,

radical/radical, radio/radio, ranch/rancho, rapid/rápido, really/realmente, region/region, regular/regular, religion/religion, restaurant/restaurante, retire/retirar, reunion/reunión, revision/revision, rich/rico, ritual/ritual, rock/roca, route/ruta, rural/rural,

secret/secreto, secular/secular, sentimental/sentimental, serial/serial, series/serie, sofa/sofá, sexual/sexual, similar/similar, simple/simple, singular/singular, solar/solar, solid/sólido, special/especial, study/estudiar, superficial/superficial, superior/superior, supermarket/supermercado, surprise/sorpresa, station/estación,

taxi/taxi, telephone/teléfono, terrible/terrible, terror/terror, theater/teatro, theory/teoría, tolerance/tolerancia, tomato/tomate, total/total, totally/totalmente, tourist/turista, traffic/tráfico, transcendental/transcendental, trap/trapar, triple/triple, tropical/tropical, trumpet/trompeta, tube/tubo,

uniform/uniforme, unilateral/unilateral, union/unión, universal/universal, usual/usual, usually/usualmente,

valid/válido, vegetables/vegetales, verbal/verbal, version/versión, vertical/vertical, violin/violín, visit/visitar, visual/visual, vital/vital, volleyball/voleibol, vote/votar, vulgar/vulgar, vulnerable/vulnerable.

(Some Spanish forms of the cognates change endings based on their gender, such as 'activo' and 'activa,' which ends with an 'o' when modifying a masculine noun and ends with an 'a' when modifying a feminine noun).

Appendix 3

False Cognates

False cognates are (English words that appear to be the same or similar to Spanish words but have different meanings

***

In this section, many false cognates are listed. These Spanish words are followed by their meanings in Spanish. Again, the Spanish definition of the word is different from the meaning of the English word that is spelled identically or similarly to the Spanish word.

***

False Cognates (Spanish word followed by its definition in Spanish): A partial list, listed alphabetically

actual means current, actualmente means currently, advertencia means warning, apologia means defense, arena means sand, argumento means reasoning, asesino means killer, asistencia means attendance, asistir means to attend,

bachillerato means high school diploma, billón means trillion, bizarro means valiant, blanco means white, blindar means to shield, bufete means desk,

campo means countryside, cargo means position or post, carpeta means folder, carrera means race or journey, carta means letter, chocar means to crash, colegio means high school, colorado means red, complexión means constitution or temperament, compromiso means commitment, conductor means driver, contester means to answer, copa means glass, culto means educated,

damnicado means victim, decepción means disappointment, desgracia means misfortune, despertar means to wake up, destitudo means dismissed, educado means polite, discutir means to debate,

educación means upbringing, embarazada means pregnant, emocionante means exciting, eventual means temporary or possible, exciter means to sexually excite, éxito means success, fábrica means factory, falta means absence, fastidioso means annoying, firma means signature, fútbol means soccer,

grabar means to save, gracioso means funny, grosería means rudeness,

humor means mood,

idioma means language, ignorer means to be unaware,

largo means long, jubilación means retirement, lectura means reading material, letra means letter of the alphabet, librería means bookstore,

mama means breast, marca means brand, mayor means larger or older, molestar means to annoy,

negocio means business, nombre means name, noticia means news,

ocasión means opportunity, once means eleven,

pan means bread, papa means potato, pariente means a close relative, patron means boss or pattern, preservativo means condom, pretender means to claim,

quitar means to take away,

real means loyal, realizar means to fulfill, receta means recipe, red means network, revolver means to turn over, ropa means clothes,

sano means healthy, sensible means sensitive, sobre means on or above or over, sopa means soup, soportar means to carry, suceso means event, suceder means to happen or follow,

trampa means trap, tuna means pear,

ultimamante means lately, ultimo means last,

vaso means glass.

Appendix 4

Spanish Vowel Sounds

As in English, there are five vowels in Spanish: a, e, i, o, u. Unlike English, each vowel has only one basic sound.

***

The letter 'a' makes the vowel sound heard in the English words 'ah' and 'mama,' and is one of several sounds the letter 'a' makes in English.

The letter 'e' makes the 'long a' vowel sound heard in the English word 'bake,' and is another one of several sounds the letter 'a' makes in English.

The letter 'i' makes the 'long e' vowel sound heard in the English word 'bee,' and is one of several sounds the letter 'e' makes in English.

The letter 'o' makes the 'long o' vowel sound heard in the English word 'go,' and is one of several sounds the letter 'o' makes in English.

The letter 'u' makes the 'oo' vowel sound heard in the English word 'student,' and is one of several sounds the letter 'u' makes in English

All five Spanish vowel sounds are heard in several Spanish words including the Spanish word for a bat, which is 'murciélago,' and the Spanish word for aeronautical, which is 'aeronaútica.'

For a description of all the letter's sounds in Spanish, see Appendix 1.

Appendix 5

The Parts of Speech

The eight parts of speech in English and Spanish are noun, pronoun, verb, adjective, adverb, conjunction, preposition, and interjection.

***

By definition: A noun is the name of a person (man, woman, child), place (city, country, continent), thing (book, pencil, car), or idea (freedom, love, fear). Nouns can be common, as in the previous examples, or they can be proper which name specific nouns and begin with a capital letter in English and in Spanish. An example of a proper noun is Robert while its common noun equivalent is man.

***

A pronoun takes the place of a noun. (The complete list of pronouns includes the following: all, another, any, anybody, anyone, anything, both, each, each other, either, everybody, everyone, everything, few, he, her, hers, herself, him, himself, his, I, it, its, itself, many, me, mine, more, most much, myself, neither, no one, nobody, none, nothing, one, one another, other, others, ours, ourselves, several, she, some, somebody someone, something, that, their, theirs, them, themselves, these, they, this, those, us, we, what, whatever, which, whichever, who, whoever, whom, whose, you, your, yours, yourself, yourselves).

***

A verb is an action word (read, write, study) or a state of being or auxiliary verb. (The auxiliary verbs 'am, is, are' are a brief example while the more exhaustive list includes the following auxiliary verbs: am, are, be, being, been, can, could, do, does, did, has, have, had, is, may, might, must, shall, should, was, were, will, would). The auxiliary verbs can stand alone (such as the word 'is') or be part of a verb phrase to indicate the tense of the action verb (such as the verb phrase 'is writing'). Of importance: an infinitive is a basic form of a verb in English and in Spanish. In English, infinitives are the word 'to' plus the action word as in the infinitive 'to speak.' In Spanish, infinitives are one word and end with the letters '– ar,' '-ir,' or '-er.' Various verb forms are developed from them. (Examples: 'hablar' is the Spanish infinitive which means the English infinitive 'to speak'; 'escribir' is the Spanish infinitive which means the English infinitive 'to write'; 'leer' is the Spanish infinitive which means the English infinitive 'to read.')

***

An adjective describes or modifies a noun or a pronoun (intelligent, studious, tall), and can be used with auxiliary verbs as opposed to action verbs (he is intelligent), and they can have degrees such as tall, taller, tallest or intelligent, more intelligent, most intelligent (he is taller than Robert is).

***

An adverb can describe or modify a verb (frequently, happily, kindly). Adverbs describe action verbs as opposed to auxiliary verbs. Most adverbs end in the letters –ly. Additionally, many adverbs are formed by adding –ly to an adjective (frequent, frequently). An adverb can also describe an adjective (quite, more, too; such as 'quite talkative'); and an adverb can describe another adverb (very, rather, most; such as 'she sings very well' in which the adverb 'very' describes or modifies the adverb 'well' which describes the verb 'sings'). Like adjectives, adverbs can also have degrees such as slow, slower, slowest or sincerely, more sincerely, most sincerely. A good way of identifying an adverb is to consider how they often answer the questions: How? (quickly or slowly). When? (tomorrow or today). Where? (there or here). To what extent? (very or extremely). Adverbs can also express affirmation (definitely), frequency (often), manner that something is done (defensively), negation (not), qualifier (however), summation (therefore), time (later). Adverbs ending in –ly in English are commonly spelled with –mente at the end of the Spanish word equivalent (slowly/lentamente).

***

A conjunction is a connecting word (and, or, but). It can connect words (boy and girl), phrases (to the school or to the playground), sentences (He is in fifth grade, and he is in the school band).

***

A preposition shows the relationship between two words in a sentence (in, such as 'the book is in my briefcase;' on, such as 'the book is on my briefcase;' next to, such as 'the book is next to my briefcase').

Prepositions are at the beginning of prepositional phrases, which contain a noun or pronoun at the end and may have adjectives between the preposition at the beginning of the prepositional phrase and the noun or pronoun at the end. In addition, a prepositional phrase may end with a gerund, which is a verb that ends with -ing in English and therefore can be used as a noun (swimming, studying, reading). In Spanish, gerunds end with –ando or –iendo or –yendo (nadando/swimming, estudiando/studying, leyendo/reading.)

A prepositional phrase may also end with a clause, which is a group of words containing a subject and predicate and can express a complete thought. There are four types of clauses: main or independent clause ('Bill dropped the ball'), subordinate or dependent clause (when he knocked, as in 'I answered the door when he knocked'; adjective or relative clause (that Scott attends, as in 'The Spanish class that Scott attends is a good class); and noun clause (whichever class you attend, as in 'Whichever class you attend is fine with me'). A noun clause acts as a noun and can begin with words such as the following: how, that, what, whatever, who, whoever, whom, whomever, why. Just as nouns, noun clauses can act as subjects, direct objects, indirect objects, predicate nominatives, or objects of a preposition. The common prepositions are: about, above, across, after against, along, among, around, at, because of, before, behind, below, beneath, beside, besides, between, beyond, but, by, concerning, despite, down, during, except, excepting, for, from, in, in front of, in spite of, inside, into, like, near, of, off, on, onto, out, outside, over, past, regarding, since, through, throughout, to, toward, under, underneath, until, up, upon, up to, with, within, without, with regard to , with respect to. Some of the words, which are commonly used as prepositions, can be used as other parts of speech as well (example: the word 'up' can be used as an adverb to indicate where, as in the expression 'look up').

***

An interjection is an abrupt remark that shows strong feeling (wow, whew, uh-oh). A list of interjections includes: aha, ahem, ahh, ahoy, alas, arg, aw, gam, bingo, blah, boo, bravo, brrr, cheers, congratulations, dang, drat, darn, duh, eek, eh, encore, gee, gee whiz, golly, goodbye, goodness, good grief, gosh, ha ha, hallelujah, hello, hey, hmm, holy cow, huh, hurray, no, oh, oh dear, oh my, oh well, oops, ouch, ow, phew, phooey, pow, shh, thanks, there, uh-huh, uh-oh, ugh, well, whew, whoa, whoops, wow, yeah, yes, yikes, yippee, yo, yuck.

Conclusion

As one who may be learning English from a Spanish-speaking base or learning Spanish from an English-speaking base, please send comments or suggestions regarding the similarities and differences between the two languages. The first publication of this book was in July of 2017 as an e-book. The most recent update occurred in September of 2019 when the print edition was made available. The author's email address is teacherpaulson@yahoo.com.

Scott Paulson has two other books about the English and Spanish languages, which are:

- English to Spanish Translations for Contemporary Conversation
- Christmas Words and Phrases in English and Spanish: Palabras y Frases Navideñas en Inglés y Español

Scott Paulson

Made in the USA
Monee, IL
06 May 2020

30033747R00025

Language learners who learn English from a Spanish language background, or vice versa, benefit greatly from knowing the many similaritities as well as the challenging differences between the two languages.

Scott Paulson

ISBN 9781694621788

90000

9 781694 621788